# THUNDER OF THE MUSTANGS

### LEGEND AND LORE OF THE WILD HORSES

## EDITED BY MARK SPRAGG

SIERRA CLUB BOOKS

A TEHABI BOOK

"The Woman and the Horse" as told by "Assiniboine" from *The Last Best Place, A Montana Anthology.* Edited by William Kittredge and Annick Smith, University of Washington Press, Seattle, and in cooperation with the Montana Historical Society. Copyright ©1988. The Assiniboine legend is in public domain.

J. Frank Dobie, "The Pacing White Steed of the Prairies" is an excerpt from *I'll Tell You a Tale* by J. Frank Dobie. Copyright ©1931 by the Southwest Press. Reprint by permission of Little, Brown and Company.

Ben K. Green, an excerpt from *A Thousand Miles of Mustangin'* by Ben K. Green, Northland Press, Flagstaff, Arizona, copyright © 1972. Permission by Northland Press.

Verlyn Klinkenborg, "The Mustang Myth," appearing in *Audubon* magazine, January-February 1994. Excerpt reprinted in this abridged form with permis-sion by Verlyn Klinkenborg.

Charles M. Russell, "The Horse," an excerpt from *Trails Plowed Under* by Charles M. Russell. Doubleday & Company, Inc. a division of Bantam Doubleday Dell Publishing Group, Inc. Copyright © 1927. Used by permission of Doubleday, a division of Bantam Doubleday Dell Publishing Group, Inc.

Library of Congress Cataloging-in-Publication Data
Spragg, Mark, 1952-
        Thunder of the Mustangs : legend and lore of the wild horses / edited by Mark Spragg. — 1st ed.
            p.        cm.
        ISBN 0-87156-974-4 (cloth: alk. paper)
            1. Wild horses—West (U.S.)  2. Wild horses—West (U.S.)—
—Folklore.  3. Wild horses—West (U.S.)—Pictorial works.  4. Mustang.  5. Mustang—Pictorial works.
    SF360.3.U6S67  1997
    599.665'5'0978—dc21
                                                                    97-16759
                                                                    CIP

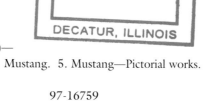

*Thunder of the Mustangs* was conceived and produced by Tehabi Books. http://www.tehabi.com
Nancy Cash–*Managing Editor;* Laura Georgakakos–*Manuscript Editor;* Kathi George-*Copy Proofer;* Sarah Morgans-*Editorial Assistant;* Sam Lewis–*Webmaster;* Andy Lewis–*Art Director;* Tom Lewis–*Editorial and Design Director;* Sharon Lewis–*Controller;* Chris Capen–*President.*

Sierra Club Books and Tehabi Books, in association with The Basic Foundation, a not-for-profit organization whose primary mission is reforestation, will facilitate the planting of two trees for every one tree used in the manufacture of this book. This edition is printed on acid-free paper that meets the American National Standards Institute z39.48 Standard.

Printed in Hong Kong through Dai Nippon. First edition 1997            10 9 8 7 6 5 4 3 2 1

# CONTENTS

*Mark Spragg*
REMEMBERING
WILDNESS
13

*Charles M. Russell*
THE HOSS
21

*J. Frank Dobie*
WIND-DRINKER
29

*Mark Spragg*
WINTERING
41

*Verlyn Klinkenborg*
WILD HORSES
53

*Assiniboine Tale*
THE WOMAN WHO
MARRIED THE HORSE
65

*Dayton O. Hyde*
THE APPY MARE
75

*Ben K. Green*
MUSTANGIN'
87

*Laura Bell*
FERAL HEART
99

*Lynne Bama*
ROUNDUP!
109

CONTRIBUTORS
120

INTRODUCTION BY

MARK SPRAGG

# REMEMBERING
# WILDNESS

THE MODERN HORSE WAS introduced to the North American continent in the early 1600s. Transported by the Spanish, he came as a slave to conquest and exploration. He did not arrive to farm or herd, he arrived to make war, and many thousands of his kind did not survive the transport. If the voyage was slowed by storm the horses often starved to death. If water was rationed they were thrown overboard and drowned. It was not uncommon for those that endured the Atlantic crossing to be killed in battle, or more commonly, slaughtered for food. And still the horse flourished in the New World. From southern Mexico to the plains of what would become the American West the horse animated a pedestrian's continent.

For the most part they were a mixture of Barb, Arabian, and Andalusian blood. They were bred for speed, endurance, beauty. They were intelligent and loyal. To some the horse was simply a "big dog"; a carrier of chattel. To others an extension of spirit. To all transportation. The horse reinvented the lives of virtually every native culture of the New World. Sport was altered, war and hunting enhanced, territory extended beyond what was previously imagined. (Once mounted, it is reported that the Blackfeet raided as far south as northern Mexico from their homeland in northern Montana.)

The horse represented literally a live coinage: traded, hoarded, stolen. His worth, however, was in relationship to his ownership. Gone wild he was worthless unless captured. For nearly four centuries he escaped

*Extremely domineering by nature, a stallion maintains control over his mares by herding and harassing them almost constantly.*

his masters into feralness. And as the Native American peoples were subjugated by disease, war, and duplicity, and then imprisoned on reservations, much of their stock swelled the already burgeoning herds of wild horses. It is estimated that by the 1860s, in the Mexican and American West, there roamed herds totaling perhaps two million mustangs.

The wild horse, and the attempts at his recapture have provided the West with its lore of the mustang. Most of the stories are told from the point of view of the cowboy and caballero; a few Native American myths have been gathered. All of the stories have to do with wildness.

It is that idea of wildness that interests me. The stories we own of domesticated animals have to do with loyalty, service, occasional inventiveness, and stamina. But the myths we create around freedom have to do with admiration and alchemy. The horse as a free mustang may be portrayed as foe, bandit, as prince or magician, but not as slave. The mustang has been romanticized and hated, but he has not been ignored. Where he exists today he is both idealized and hunted.

My initiation with the wild horse had to do with a small band of mustangs in the McCullough Peaks northwest of Cody, Wyoming. We had turned out our bunch to winter in the Peaks and returned the next spring to gather them. After two days' work we were still short ten horses, finally finding them absorbed by one of the wild bands. I thought it romantic. I could hardly wait to recapture them and, of course, the dozen or so mustangs they ran with.

I spent a mostly sleepless night imagining myself aboard a wild stallion. I saw myself as handsomer, taller, windblown, my nostrils, and my wild horse's nostrils, flared in rebellion. In my fantasy we were spirits that would be reunited. If ever a boy was born to ride a mustang it was me.

Three days later the romance had worn thin. My brother and I had ridden half a dozen good horses to the point of exhaustion to cut out the ones that carried our brand. And we only accomplished the task at all through the luck of running into an abandoned and derelict corral, barely enough of a barrier to make our stock remember domesticity. It was not sufficient for the mustangs. They were crazy with their liberty. The ran into poles until the wood splintered. They careened over cutbanks. Their mouths frothed. Their eyes rolled white with fear. But we had come close to them. We had smelled them and seen them as real. We would recognize them forever as wild animals; as gaunt, big-boned, badly formed, and scarred. The band's sorrel and cream-blotched stud swung a giant skull that looked forged in a mill. I was disillusioned to the point of tears. The experience left me not caring if I ever saw another wild horse. My fantasies had been so damaged that the mustang dropped in my estimation to nothing more heroic than a large insect. My gods had turned up with hooves of clay.

The next summer, a friend of my father's left with us a usable horse, once wild, and I made a point of ignoring him. He was a seven-year-old who had been free until he was three. I treated him like the thing he was: a half-breed fallen into the space between my dreams and reality. He did not compare to the mustang stallion that once held my fantasies, in fact, he was an example of what had ruined them. He was a bay, short-coupled, and moderately muscled. His neck was unattractively thick because he had remained a stud until his capture. I thought of him as an inadequate bantam weight too used up to stay in his racket. His name was Dutch.

"Most of the sonsofbitches can eat out of a fifty-five gallon drum and you can see their ears and eyes," said one of our hired hands about wild horses.

"Not Dutch," I said. Not meaning to defend him, but he did have an intelligent-looking head.

Still, I made no move to ride him. I didn't give him so much as a second glance. But fortunately the necessities of a ranch almost always override our personal bigotries. It was the necessity of difficult work that reinvented my idea of the wild horse.

In the fall, on trips back and forth over the Continental Divide, we ran loose stock for fresh mounts. Halfway through one of those trips my handsomer horse played out in the snow and I was forced to get Dutch under me. I had fallen behind the pack string and he was there to let me catch him.

Within ten miles I'd fallen in love. Whether I was a fickle boy, or insightful, I at least knew when I was well-mounted. Dutch had heart. He was intelligent and inventive. He solved problems, remained level-headed in bad situations, had a sense of humor, and operated at full throttle. Yet he made it clear that he didn't work for his rider, but if ridden well, was willing to form a partnership. I didn't ride another horse until we turned them out for the winter. My idea of the mustang was once again revived. This time in the body of a tough, little bay gelding. He made me believe again in my own sense of wildness. I wish I still had him around.

Every essay in this collection has found a way to resurrect my memories of Dutch, both actual and fantasized. Dayton Hyde, Ben Green, Frank Dobie, and Charlie Russell have lived the cowboy life. Their firsthand experiences with wild horses are demonstrated in their stories: Dobie's deft handling of myth, Green's no-nonsense storytelling, Russell's campfire humor, and Dayton Hyde's true fondness and reverence for the animals he deals with daily.

Laura Bell has lived among wild horses for months at a time, out with her sheep, grazing mustang range, listening for their presence in the night. Lynne Bama chronicles the end of a band's wildness, the literal end of a stallion's life, and—like Laura Bell—finds an appreciation for the unbridled parts of herself. Both writers give us stories that are lyrical, and yet as rugged as the Wyoming landscape. Bama's essay strikes a chord of contemplative concern.

I have included the Assiniboine tale for two reasons. Firstly, because I find it lovely, and secondly, because I wish it not to be seen as allegory. I urge the reader to believe it—even for a moment.

Verlyn Klinkenborg's essay struck me because of its honesty, beautifully precise language, and finally, its assertion that humans and horses form a single and inseparable community.

All of these men and women know horses, both wild and tame. In their stories we are reminded that across the terrain of the heart runs a horse that utterly shuns domestication. I hope that in these stories you glimpse that mustang, hear his hoofstrikes, feel his breath, smell the salt of his exertion, and taste the ineffable joy of his freedom. **,,**

**W**ild horses may carry a variety of natural markings—like the snip, which is any marking extending vertically between the forehead and

the nostril, and the blaze, which is a broader vertical marking extending the length of the face.

# THE HOSS

"I READ IN THE PAPERS A WHILE back where there's 70,000 wild hosses on the ranges of Montana," says Rawhide Rawlins. "They say these animals are a menace to stockmen. Mebbe this is right, but I think it would bother this old state to round up that many tame ones.

"A few years ago a hoss was considered kind of handy to have around. He was needed everywhere and used all ways. Up hill or down, mud or dust, he worked. They made no good roads for him. There's not a city in mighty near the whole world he didn't help build. There's a few icebound countries where the hoss don't live, and in these same lands it ain't easy for humans to live.

"This last war was a machine-made hell, but I doubt if it could have been win without hosses, an' the same kind that some folks say is a menace to men now. There was thousands of branded hosses died with our fighters on the other side. The range hoss was God-made, an' like all of His makin', the best. These hosses cost the man that branded an' claimed 'em nothing. They lived on the grass an' water the Almighty gave 'em.

"Many thousand years ago, when folks was all a-foot, lizards, horned toads, an' bullfrogs measured from thirty to 100 feet in length an' stood from forty to sixty hands. Besides these, there was tigers and laffin' hyenas that would eat an elephant for breakfast. From what I've read, in the days I'm talkin' about man wasn't much, an' he sure lived simple. A good, stout cave was his home. He fed mostly on bugs an' snails, an' a grasshopper that happened to 'light anywhere

**W**ild horses in the western states still have much in common with their sixteenth-century Spanish ancestors.

near him or his family was out of luck. Sometimes some real game gent would slip out with his stone tomahawk an' bring back a skunk or two. Then's when they pulled a regular feed, but there wasn't no set date for these feasts, an' they mostly came far apart. With a hyena that weighed seven ton a-laffin' around the door, man loved his home, an' Maw never worried about where Paw was.

"But one day one of these old home-livers was sunnin' himself an' layin' for a grasshopper, when he looks down from his ledge to the valley below where all these animals is busy eatin' one another an' notices one species that don't take no part in this feast, but can out-run an' out-dodge all others. This cave man is progressive, an' has learned to think. He sees this animal is small compared to the rest, an' ain't got no horns, tusks, or claws, eatin' nothin' but grass. There's other grass-eaters, but they all wear horns that don't look good to Mister Cave Man.

"He remembers when his Maw used to pack him on her back. Bein' a lazy gent he's lookin' for somethin' easy, an' he figgers that if he could get this hornless animal under him, he could ride once more like he did in his childhood. Right then is when man starts thinkin' of somethin' besides eatin'.

"Not far from the cave there's a trail where herds of hosses come to water, so one day Mister Man climbs into a tree that hangs over the trail, an' with a grapevine loop he snares one of these animals. But he finds out that though this beast ain't got horns or claws, he's mighty handy with all four feet, and when Paw sneaks home that evenin' he's got hoof marks all over him an' he ain't had a ride yet. Sore as he is, he goes back next day an' tries

again. About the sixth day this poor hoss is so starved that Mister Man gets up to him, an' tyin' a strip of bark to his under jaw an' another around his belly, he steps across the hoss. The bronc sinks his head an' goes in the air. Mister Man stays, but he breaks all the rules in a ridin' contest of to-day. He don't pull leather, but tears all the mane out from ears to withers, an' that bark handhold of his is all that keeps the hoss from unloadin' him. A few days later his bronc is plumb gentle. Paw mounts, goes out an' with a stone-headed spear kills a wild cow, an' he comes back to the cave with the hide an' more meat than the folks ever seen before. The family is so pleased with this useful pet that they bring him in the cave nights, an' all get busy pullin' grass for him.

"Mister Man finds that with four legs under him instead of two, he can ride rings around them big lizards, an' there ain't any of them claw-wearin', tusk-bearin' critters can overtake him. The old gent snares more hosses, an' it ain't long till the whole family's hoss-back. When this bunch starts out, armed an' mounted, they sure bring home the bacon. Meat—I'd tell a man. This cave looks an' smells like a packin' plant before the pure food law. It's now mankind sheds the leaf garments of old Grand-dad Adam an' starts wearin' new clothes.

"Paw's wearin' a head-an'-tail cowskin'; the boys has a yearlin' robe apiece. Maw an' the girls wouldn't be in style at all these days. Mebbe it's modesty—it might be the chill in the weather—but they're sure covered from ears to heels in deer an' elk skins, an' from that day to just lately man never knowed whether his sweetheart was knock-kneed or bowlegged.

"Since that old bug-eater snared that first cayuse, his

descendants have been climbin', an' the hoss has been with 'em. It was this animal that took 'em from a cave. For thousands of years the hoss an' his long-eared cousins furnished all transportation on land for man an' broke all the ground for their farmin'. He has helped build every railroad in the world. Even now he builds the roads for the automobile that has made him nearly use-less, an' I'm here to tell these machine-lovers that it will take a million years for the gas wagon to catch up with the hoss in what he's done for man. Today some of these auto drivers want to kill him off to make fertilizer out of his body. Mebbe I'm sentimental, but I think it's a damned hard finish for one that has been as good a friend to man as the hoss." ,,

**A** *wild horse with its strong, sturdy legs and thick, shaggy coat is well suited for the brutal wilderness range.*

**T**he Spanish mustang was a part of early American history and helped settle the West.

**A** *mixture of white and black, the gray is usually born a solid color or almost a solid color, and turns lighter with age.*

**A** *strong bond between the mare and her foal is an important factor in the foal's survival.*

EXCERPTED FROM *THE PACING WHITE STEED OF THE PRAIRIES* BY
J. FRANK DOBIE

# WIND-DRINKER

EVERY SECTION OF THE MUSTANG world had its notability—the subject of campfire talk and the object of chases. Supreme above all superiors was the Pacing White Mustang. A superb stallion of one region in the beginning, he became the composite of all superb stallions. The loom of human imagination wove him into the symbol of all wild and beautiful and fleet horses. Riders everywhere over a continent of free grass came to know of him and many to dream of capturing him. His fame spread beyond the Atlantic. He passed from the mortality of the bounded and aging into the immortality of the legended.

The great horse went under varying names—the White Steed of the Prairies, the Pacing White Stallion, the White Mustang, the Ghost Horse of the Plains. His fire, grace, beauty, speed, endurance, and intelligence were exceeded only by his passion for liberty. He paced from the mesas of Mexico to the Badlands of the Dakotas and even beyond, from the Brazos bottoms of eastern Texas to parks in the Rocky Mountains.

According to some accounts, this "wind-drinker" was never caught. "He seemed to glide rather than work his legs, he went so smoothly. He did not seem to be trying to get away from his pursuers, only to lead them on. He moved like a white shadow." At one time, the mares in his bands might outnumber those of half a dozen other bands. Again, if his freedom depended upon his leaving every single follower behind, he racked on and on—alone over the prairie grasses, "like a bird flying low," "like a spirit horse"—

*The pinto has a body color with two or more spots.*

as singular in his streaming whiteness as the white whale Moby Dick, as the solitary white blackbird in a flock of thousands, as the one white buffalo of unspeakable "medicine" in an earth-darkening migration of a million.

No one of the organized hunts after him ever won the reward of dollars offered for his living body. In the fall of 1879, for example, an owner of fine race horses hired riders at Bonham, Texas, rode with them up into the Indian Territory (now Oklahoma), and there engaged a number of reservation Indians to close in on the champion racer of the unfenced world.

"The hunters found the great Mustang all right. They laid all kinds of traps for him and tried all kinds of dodges to run him down or hem him in. But when he was crowded he would break off from his *manada,* they said, and pace away like the wind. According to their report, he was not pure white but of a light cream color with snow-white mane and tail. The Indians believed him to be supernatural and called him the Ghost Horse of the Prairies or the Winged Steed. When running at a distance he showed nothing but a fast-flying snow-white mane and snow-white tail that looked like wings skimming the ground. The boys who got nearest to him said he had a piece of rawhide rope around his neck. They thought he had been snared at some watering and that the experience had helped to make him what he was—the most alert and the wildest as well as the fleetest animal in western America.

"Mustang hunters kept after him, and, according to report, he changed his range from the Washita to the South Canadian. Such a change showed wonderful cunning, for the ordinary mustang when chased would keep circling within certain limits until he was finally closed in. Some of the mustangers swore they would get the White Ghost of the Prairies even if they had to shoot him. Death from a rifle may have been his fate."

If "death from a rifle" was the uncatchable animal's "fate," he came to life somewhere else. According to one story, a vaquero not far from the Rio Grande happened to see him after he had paced for 200 miles away from a band of professional mustangers. This was away back yonder, before the Civil War. The vaquero roped him, got help from two other men, fixed a clog on one of his forefeet, and staked him so that he could not choke himself to death. When night came, he was standing where they left him, not having taken a mouthful of grass. The next day they carried a sawed-off barrel, used as a trough, within the horse's reach and filled it with water. He did not notice it. For ten days and ten nights he remained there, grass all about him, water within reach of his muzzle, without taking one bite or one swallow. Then he lay down and died.

No matter what claims may have been advanced by reputed captors or what tales rumored, the White Steed of the Prairies never surrendered. He and his kind no longer graze and watch over the wild and free world that they once dominated, but the mystery of the Ghost Horse of the Plains is not likely to vanish.

Along in the fifties, as the story goes, a fiddling, yarning character called Kentuck reached Santa Fe and threw in with an Arkansas gambler operating under the name of Jake. They heard so much talk about the White Steed of the Prairies and Jake had such a run of good luck that he decided to take his partner and hunt down the horse. He bought pack mules, everything needed for a pack trip, and four New Mexican horses of speed and endurance.

"I don't know exactly whur to hunt," Jake said, "but we'll ride on the prairies till we find the hoss or till they are burned crisp by the fires of Jedgment Day." He had a kind of fever in his mind.

They rode east on the Santa Fe Trail, and then away north of the Arkansas River; they crisscrossed the endless carpet of short buffalo grass back southward until they were on the Staked Plains of the Canadian. They shot buffaloes and lived on hump. They dodged Indians and met no white man. Wherever wild horse sign led, they followed. They saw many bands and many stallions without bands, with now and then a white or gray among them, but not the Pacing White Stallion.

Summer passed into fall and northers brought the fluting sandhill cranes. Kentuck, who had not from the start had much heart in this wild-goose chase, yearned for bed and bedwarmer in Sante Fe. The longer Jake hunted and the more mustangs he saw, the hotter he grew on the quest.

"Go back if you want," he said with a fixed hardness to his partner. "Go and rot. I hev sworn to git what I come to git. If I don't git him, I'll keep on a-hunting till the Day of Jedgment." He knew that Kentuck would not break away from his domination.

The White Pacer and the Day of Judgment seemed linked in his mind, and nothing else in it came to the surface. As winter opened, he took it into his head that the White Stallion would appear pacing out of the southwest. Whether riding or camping, he seldom looked now in another direction.

One cold, misty day, visibility cut to only a few yards, their camp backed against a rise of ground to the north, near a lake, the men huddled and pottered about a feeble fire of wet buffalo chips. They existed only to hunt on. About sunset the skies cleared. For an hour not a word had been said. Now, while Kentuck rustled for chips dry on the bottom side, Jake squatted in his serape, straining his eyes towards the southwest as if he expected to catch the movement of something no bigger than a curlew's head in the rim of grass blades. The glow of the sun had melted and a full moon was coming up in the clear sky when he yelled, "Yonder," and ran towards his staked horse.

"I supposed it was Indians and grabbed my rifle," Kentuck later told. "Then my eyes picked up the white horse. He stood there to the southwest, maybe a hundred yards off, head lifted, facing us, as motionless as a statue. In the white moonlight his proportions were all that the tales had given him. He did not move until Jake moved towards him. As I made for my horse, I saw that Jake was riding without saddle, though he had bridled his horse and held his reata. We kept our rawhide lariats well greased so that they would not get limp from water and stiffen when dry.

"The White Pacer paced east, against the moon, and against a breeze springing up. He seemed to glide rather than work his legs, he went so smoothly. He did not seem to be trying to get away, only to hold his distance. He moved like a white shadow, and the harder we rode, the more shadowy he looked."

After the run had winded his horse, Kentuck called out, "Jake, I don't like this. There's no sense to it. I'm remembering things we've both heard. Let's stop. We can't no more catch up with him than with our own shadows."

Jake had lost his hat. His long black hair was streaming back. His set features were those of a madman. He screamed out, "Stop if yer want. I've told yer I'm a-going to foller till the Day of Jedgment."

Not another word passed between the two. Kentuck did not stop. "Riding on and on out there in the middle of nowhere, not even a coyote breaking the silence, it didn't seem like this world," he said. Then he made out a long black line across the ground ahead. "It'll soon be settled now," he thought, "and we'll know whether the White Stallion can cross empty space like a ghost." Pulling back his horse, he yelled to Jake, "Watch out for the canyon—the bluff."

The word "Jedgment" came to his ears and he saw Jake using his coiled reata for a quirt. Then he disappeared over the bluff. Kentuck was watching him so intently that he did not see what became of the Pacing White Stallion.

Kentuck walked from his heaving horse to examine the canyon brink. He could hear nothing below. Downward in the moonlight he saw only jags of ground amid the stubby growth called *palo duro* (hard wood). He called, but there was no response. He hobbled his horse and about daylight found a buffalo trail leading down the turreted bluffs. Soon after sunup he came upon what was left of Jake and his horse, a full hundred feet below the jumping-off place. He did the best he could for a grave. **"**

**A** lead mare will not only determine the trails to be taken in time of crisis, but she often stands as a second sentinel to the stallion.

**W**ild horses will brave the elements, turning their backsides to the wind, rather than seek shelter.

AN ORIGINAL ESSAY BY

MARK SPRAGG

# WINTERING

THE RANCH WAS HIGH, 7,500 feet, and in every direction there was no sign of man. Thirty miles to the east, twenty south, forty west, and against my back the home mountain of Forest Service pine, spruce, and silence, contracting, cooling itself in preparation for winter's early and steadfast embrace.

When I first saw the place I knew I would take the job of populating it, become its sole human. I leaped at the chance, upward. Naive in my fantasies of solitude, and ignorant to the differences of altitude and season, I did not know that in the fall sound quickens, its edges chipped as sharp as obsidian knives. I did not know that at altitude all wounds heal slowly. My lessons began immediately.

On the morning of my second day I woke early

to an alarming and constant scream. I did not say to myself, "Those are the screams of a horse." I said nothing. The sound was as present as the shriek from some violent and angered god. I leaped from bed pulling on my clothes and ran from the house, trying ridiculously to fasten, zip, and button as I ran, but run I did, and frantically toward the sound, as I said, of screaming, because that is what it was and I did not know it was a horse until I found her.

She had gotten into the cattle-guard closest the house; all four legs of her, snapped at the knees. (A cattle-guard is very much like a thick-barred jailhouse door laid on the ground, and over a pit. It is used as a gate that does not need opening. The fence is stopped at either side of it, and you can drive your truck

*Deep snows will cause many wild horses to perish because they are unable to find food.*

through, or walk across if you are careful not to turn a foot sideways and fall in to your thighs.) She had thrashed while she screamed and blood ran from her nose and ears and barely from an eye she had beaten loose from its socket. Her leg bones had torn through her flesh, and worked as she struggled, like the jagged teeth of some demonic beast feeding on her from the earth, stopped from rising into the air by the iron bars on which she lay, losing her fight to live, breathing hard between screams, her mouth slick with a pink foam, her one good eye rolling white, but glazing rapidly in shock.

I have heard a man scream, pinned under the broken and dropped block of an oil rig—a scream of intense pain and bewilderment—a woman during a childbirth gone wrong, a mountain lion shot through the bowel, a male bald eagle broken and falling in what I imagined was a lost fight for family or sex. They were one scream. They were the scream of this horse—a sound that strips muscle from bone and leaves the listener merely skeletal and vibrating stark and white as an ivory tuning fork. The screamers must labor through the weight of their pain. The screaming, their breath gone wild, uncaged, sheering them away from consciousness.

The scream pulled me to its very center, contracted and loosed my tendons, ligaments, jerked my knees high into the air, made me generally elastic with fear, and fast. It was not a matter of wanting to witness the source of the sound. It drew me and I went, and was lucky for that. That I had to look into it.

Had I run away—had I been fortunate enough to hear this sound—become confused and turned from it, it would have crazed my core; left of me a ruined vessel. Because, and I mean this precisely, what reached my ears, what reached past them and inside of me was the sound of death, and that is a sound, that to continue meaningfully, to continue even to sleep at night, we hope to break with our chests, not our backs. Had I moved in any direction except into the sound it would have been to step into a trench; a shoulder-wide grave in which I would have run until out of wind, and aged profoundly more useless than I am. I would have instantly become a man I could not trust.

The sight of her turned me faster toward the house and I scrabbled for my pistol, gripped it as though it were the neck of a rabid dog, gripped it hard because I was alone and knew what I was about to do, and made my second sprint to her. Her cries were deeper. The ground shivered with them. Birds flew toward me in confusion. Prairie dogs scattered in a panic to avoid the slaughter they believed she heralded. I reached her, breathed in once to steady my lungs and heart and fired into her head. I had to shoot her twice so determined was her struggle, and then I walked into the sage and sat, held my palms against the earth and howled because it seemed my only adequate response. I feel that that unexpected sound of grieving saved my life, saved me from going with her; breaking through the thin and penetrable surface that holds us away from our individual deaths. I sat, I think, for an hour and then walked to the house and backed my little four-wheel-drive to her body.

I sawed through the ruined bone and tissue and hide at her knees, worked her legs from the cattle-guard and laid them in the back of the Scout, and pulled a length of chain to her. I looped the chain around her neck, hooking it snugly under the ridge of her jawbone. I circled the free end over the trailer hitch and eased out in the lowest gear. The chain bit solidly, her head held fast, and I dragged the amputated corpse a mile from the buildings, sliding her into a deep ravine, her legs tossed on top of her, where she would bloat and rot and feed every manner of predator that caught her scent.

Within a month, a rain and two wet snows faded her blood to rust, to ocher, blending it finally into the dark, brown ground across which she'd run. Her scream remained, absorbed by the side of the mountain, held as edged and brittle and wracked as the day it had torn itself loose from her, the mare, a bay, a horse unused to the inventiveness of men. I wired plywood over the cattle-guards and put in gates so as not to trap more than just the first.

The snows came finally and did not go, and closed the road and left me up at this high place completely unsurprised. I had filled a freezer and pantry to feed my winter cloister, hired by an absent owner to guard against accident: frozen water lines, theft. I kept the buildings heated so they would not have to constrict to thirty-five below, and spilled hay to the fifty grown-fierce horses that prowled the ridges blown free of snow. The raptors, the coyotes, and these inbred horses were my company.

The horses had never been touched, fourth generation wild, their mistress—the woman from whom the ranch had been purchased—in her eighties, preferring them free from labor, contracting for their life tenancy. I had seen them, twice before the snow, catch a coyote out too far from cover, encircling the quick gray dog, and by sheer force of number, each angle vec-

tored by a striking hoof, hack the little predator to a mess of trampled bone and pulp.

I knew it skittered in their minds that I could go the way of a coyote. When mounted they where as hard to find as deer, but when I walked out through the sage they became curious, as tigers do. Half a dozen times I'd bounced an armful of rocks off their sides, and waved my coat above my head, and bluffed the mob of them apart. When the cold pushed the songbirds south and froze the fist-sized stones into the mountainside I walked less. And when the snow was deep and I was out on snowshoes in a moon so bright my shadow followed black, I kept to the edge of timber. I felt they blamed me for the mare.

The months passed and I went about my chores and there were not so many. I had taken the job, as I said, to be alone, away from people, to paint a little, to write, but the clinching reason, to be alone. I'd taken precautions: no radio, no television (reception would have been doubtful), no phone, no record player, no chance to be tempted back to lower elevations. I vowed that I would not lose altitude. I put my watch in a drawer in October and did not rummage for it until spring. I did not break my vow.

There was a month of dislocation and then I lined out and worked sixteen, sometimes twenty hours at a stretch. Would at times, the best I could gauge, sleep a day and a half and wake in the night and wash and go to work. I kept the feral horses fed and made drawings and stories and as time lost all its rote and civilized boundaries, became a whole and seasonal thing, I grew more comfortably wild myself. I ate when I was very hungry, I watched the mountains for, at times, a complete revolution of the planet, and observed myself grow increasingly quiet, and more gentle. The untamed lives that surrounded me moved closer to my heat, my pulse, at times mice and squirrels sat on my knees, not all together comfortably, but they came that close—or, I to them.

One day out I leaned against a fir to watch my breath freeze and drop away, and found a great horned owl perched inches from my head. He looked into my eyes and seemed to nod, to say in gesture, that for a man I was bending toward a rightness. I closed my eyes until I could hear him breathe, and opened them and it had gotten dark, but he'd not flown, and I moved stiffly toward my heated house to warm my hands and feet, smiling in the dark.

Through all those frozen months—had I used a watch and calendar to keep them months—the mountain sent back through every pore of me the dying horse's scream. Day and night her last and desperate sound of pain silently scoured me clean, loosening childhood, shattering thoughts of future when they came, suspending me in each moment's beauty, remarkably without sentiment.

I often, toward the end of winter, would lie in bed and try to reckon whether I had just waked from a dream of words and drawings, or whether I had stretched myself down from standing, having tired of a day of making stories in the cold. The mare's scream kept cleaning me, until finally, and only once, I heard the Earth whisper that she did not care, that it did not matter whether I was awake or soundly slept when creation came, only that I was clean enough to hear the text. I often wonder whether I had gone mad, or gone completely sane.

Somewhere close to the vernal equinox, the snow puddling at the height of day, and freezing bright at night, I woke and thought I heard footsteps somewhere over me. Most of this house, for which I was paid to care, was built above my bed and on its walls hung several dozen precious paintings. The owner thought them part of him; a wardrobe of celebrated canvases left high on a Wyoming mountain.

I slipped out of bed and was in the hall, my left foot on the bottom stair, and looked to my right and watched in wonder as my hand thumbed back the hammer of the magnum pistol that it held. I'd fired it last into a screaming horse. I edged up, and from room to room, the gun held out in front of me. It caught the light of a waning moon as did everything in front of me, slicing the whole of the house into a thousand shadowscapes.

I searched the house down to the last room. I stood at its threshold convinced I'd notched myself to the nub of death, convinced the assassin-thief I knew I'd heard waited comfortably for me to walk into his trap and die. I nearly pissed myself with fear.

I kept my back to the wall and eased into the room and there he was, across from me, cornered and raising a gun held in both hands, both eyes locked on the target of my heart. He did not fire, because I did not fire, recognizing in the last fragment of a second before I squeezed the bullet free that the man I faced was my twin, come to sack the place dressed as I was, in his best white cotton underwear. I slid down the wall, and sat and stared across my knees at the reflection of myself caught in the gathered moonlight of a floor-to-ceiling mirror flown in that summer from the north of Italy. The house seemed suddenly gone empty.

Except for my reflection I had no proof that I was there. The mirror was only lit by moonlight, and for months my only conversation, an animal's last cry of pain.

I snowshoed out the next afternoon, 2,000 feet down to a valley already free of snow. I cut the two-lane at dusk and caught a ride to town with an aged rancher known regionally for his total lack of irony. We did not speak, except for my request to be dropped at a roadside tavern at the city's farthest outskirt.

There was a blaring band and the place was packed. I forced my way to the bar and shouted my order and thought the noise of the people might shatter me. I tucked a six-pack of cans against my ribs and strained back through the crowd and out. A girl my age knelt to the side of the entrance, where the dark began, and vomited. She dropped to her side, asleep, and I covered her with my denim jacket and walked behind the building, where there was just a ledge fifty feet across to the lip of a canyon, water-carved when this quiet plain grazed the beginning herds of horses. Now, there is a bar and this place to be careful behind it on a dark night when trying to find the parking lot.

I sat on the canyon's edge, my feet dangling hundreds of feet above the Shoshone River, and drank, one at a time, my cans of pale, weak beer. The moon was high and shone on the strand of river and in a mottled smear of cloud to the south, and brightly to the west on the white and frozen mountain where I had been so long alone.

I felt the throb of the music drop through into the porous rock on which I sat. It climbed the column of my spine—I thought that night—in a single-minded effort to reconstruct me more social. There was, too, making its way into my bones, drunken laughter, voices edged in threat, murmurings of sex. I drew up my knees and hugged them and dropped my forehead on their caps, my eyes closed, and even though I cannot hold a tune knew that what my ears heard in this sad music was the harmony of a dying horse. It was a slower scream, and many voiced, but filled with pain—the slower music of a slower death.

I stood unsteadily and started upriver and away from town. I smiled into the moon as though the single eye of a single owl, and knew that had I fired the night before into the mirrored image of myself, they would have found the gun and glass, painted black to reflect the light, but they would not have found the place where I had gone, dropped noiselessly down a winter's shaft of gathered quietude. ❞

*Competition for mares is violent between stallions who shriek, snort, and bite at each other.*

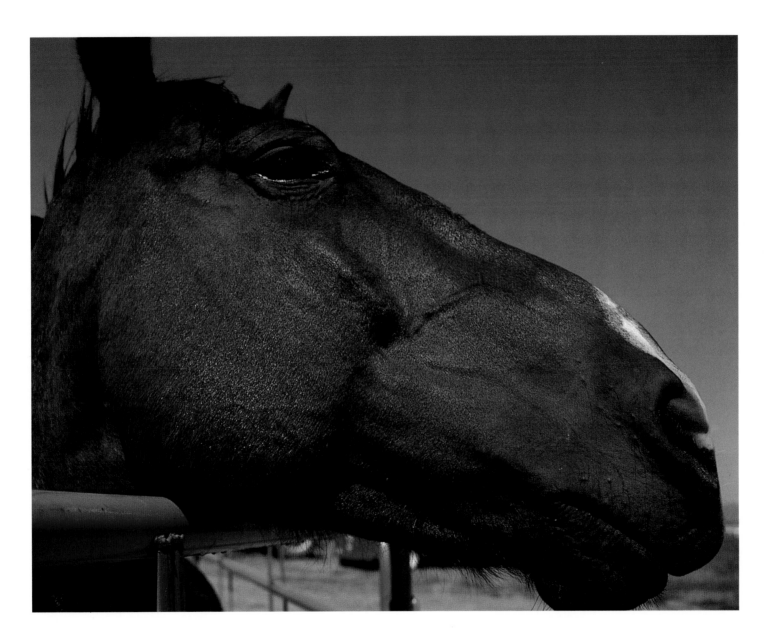

*Certain horses are born with specific identifying characteristics—like this Roman nose, the convex areas between the eyes and the muzzle.*

*A buckskin is a form of a dun horse with yellowish or gold body color. Its mane and tail are black, and it usually has black on its lower legs with a dorsal stripe.*

*The protector of his band, the wary stallion will test water holes and trails for signs of danger, keeping his mares from falling into traps.*

EXCERPTED FROM *THE MUSTANG MYTH* BY

# VERLYN KLINKENBORG

# WILD HORSES

WE WERE NOT MEMBERS OF HIS congregation, and the Reverend Floyd Schwieger was not in his pulpit. But with only his voice, which has a touch of bell bronze in it, Schwieger held us below the crest of a windy ridgeline near the top of Pryor Mountain on the border of Montana and Wyoming. He understood our excitement, for he had been coming to this mountain every week for nearly thirty years, sometimes to think, sometimes to write sermons. "Please," he said, "walk slowly once we get over the top, and stop if you see them moving away." In most small towns you can find several men and women—the schoolhouse activists, the salespeople, the toastmaster elite—who are as well-spoken, as authoritative as an ordained minister like Schwieger. But it is the minister's task to acknowledge,

publicly, the force of emotion, to accommodate it for better in places where it's so often accommodated for worse.

"Is everybody ready?" Schwieger asked. "Okay, let's go."

At his word, fifty-two men and women strung out in a line a quarter-mile long, walked up the gentle slope to the top of the ridge. On the other side, clumped and cautious, stood a small herd of wild horses, grazing each with one eye turned our way, their ears shifting back and forth. The foals and one of the stallions in the near group turned to watch us with lifted heads, and the stallion trotted between us and his mares. The herd drifted downslope and then gathered again, held itself, and began to feed quietly. Below the horses the great wedge of Pryor Mountain fell away

*Evolving in the Americas, except for a brief absence, the wild horse has been a part of the ecological design of North America for millions of years.*

into Wyoming, into the canyon of the Bighorn River and the Bighorn Basin, into a badland etched by runoff in the years when this southern slope catches enough rain and snow to make runoff possible, and scraped by wind, of which in every year there's plenty.

Fifty-two men and women facing thirty-odd horses, perhaps 100 yards apart. This was not a roundup or a rescue or a capture. The occasion was the twenty-fifth anniversary of the Pryor Mountain National Wild Horse Range, and we were there to celebrate with our presence the presence of wild horses on ground more or less consecrated to them. Cameras clicked and whirred, and many of us wished we could have been alone on this mountaintop—alone among the horses, that is. A suppressed urge arose in some of us, too—watching the nimbleness of these small horses, the delicate beauty of these duns and grullas and blue roans and red roans and bays and blacks—the urge to own one, to saddle one, to ride one, and then to ride that one among all the rest of the band. But who can guess what everyone in that herd of humans was really thinking—the Bureau of Land Management range managers, the scientists, the citizens of nearby Lovell, the horse lovers, conservationists, cowboys, crackpots, and ministers? . . .

The night before, a large crowd had gathered under a sky of Venetian blue at an amphitheater above Horseshoe Bend on the Bighorn River. As twilight faded, a bat cast fluttering shadows against the backlit projection screen, and a veil of late-summer mosquitoes descended on us. Phillip Sponenberg, a vet-

erinary pathologist at Virginia Polytechnic Institute and an adviser to the American Livestock Breeds Conservancy, was lecturing informally, accompanied by slides, about the history and genetic makeup of the Pryor Mountain horses. Sponenberg is a tall, slender, graying man, a scientist with an air of finely calibrated patience. Over the last few years he has been conducting a census of "North American colonial Spanish horses": wild horses, loosely called Spanish mustangs, and nonwild horses whose descent can be traced by several means—including blood-typing, a study of their shape (or conformation), and existing local narratives—to the herds the Spaniards brought to this continent in the sixteenth and seventeenth centuries. Sponenberg has concluded that the Pryor Mountain horses, like those from the Cerbat Mountains in Arizona and the Sulphur Horse Management Area in Utah, show unmistakable signs of Spanish origin, the result of genetic isolation in the kind of rugged rangeland that formed our northern horizon that night.

Though Sponenberg was speaking offhandedly—"Spanish horses tend to be small," he would say, "and white people tend to like big horses"—he was telling a story whose every detail has caused debate. The ancestors of horses first evolved on the American continent in the Eocene period, sixty-five million years ago, but the last of their New World descendants died out some 8,000 years ago. (Yet despite the lack of evidence, a few people contend that horses never became extinct in America and that wild horses include "native" horses, whose history somehow reaches back to those prehistoric herds.) Horses were reintroduced to the Americas by the Spaniards, mainly from breeding ranches in the Caribbean, although Spanish horses did not begin to be scattered through the wild until the late sixteenth and early seventeenth centuries. By the mid-1800s, they may have numbered in the millions. (Yet some people, especially those who want to graze cattle instead of wild horses, maintain that all wild horses descend from ranch stock that escaped or was turned loose in the late nineteenth century and during the Depression.) The traits so obvious in the Pryor Mountain horses—small size; sloping croup; long, tapering muscles; deep body; convex head with fine, crescent nostrils—are characteristic of Spanish colonial horses. (And yet many people believe intuitively that all wild horses are inbred and badly conformed, and that inbreeding makes wild horses small.) There are many good reasons to preserve wild horses, Sponenberg argued but one of the best is to preserve genetic diversity, for the Pryor Mountain horses resemble the animals raised in Spain 500 years ago more than they resemble modern horses.

"I think they're unique," Sponenberg was saying, "and there's no reason that I can see not to save something that's unique. They're historically and culturally important. They tend to make very good riding mounts. Many people say that the horses out on the range are inbred and that's why they look the way they look. From blood-typing studies, we know that these horses are not inbred. Inbreeding does not change things, it only accentuates what's there." . . .

At Horseshoe Bend the mood of the crowd was celebratory, festive, but it was also oddly proprietary. As Sponenberg spoke, as the audience laughed at his jokes and slapped at mos-

quitoes, as the bat struggled to free itself from the persuasive illusion cast by the slide projector's lamp, I could sense the moral and aesthetic weight of the 140 wild horses that live on Pryor Mountain, just a handful of animals, really, in a horse-raising region like northern Wyoming, and only the faintest vestige of the herds that once inhabited the West. I could feel in the crowd, and could hear in their questions, a competitive zeal to represent those wild horses, to stand on their behalf, to speak for their welfare. But as welcome as that zeal was, it was a problem, too, for humans cannot represent wild horses without conceptualizing them, without making an issue of their conformation or their genes or their coloration or their history or their association with Indians or especially their freedom, their symbolic value. The critical difficulty in dealing with animals, particularly those that live apart from humans, is this: No matter how hard you try to acknowledge the intrinsic reality of their lives—what you might call the "ownness" of their existence, their self-possession—they soon become almost ghostly with abstraction. And the greatest abstraction of all is wildness. . . .

On the western plains a century and a half ago, there were no savages and there were no truly wild horses. There were perhaps millions of feral horses, small herds of which were being skillfully managed, and some skillfully bred, by Indians who had integrated the culture of horsemanship—inherited from the Spaniards along with the horse—into their own remarkable cultures. The descendants of those feral horses are the mustangs, or "wild" horses, of the modern American West.

Deciding to call wild horses *feral* is not just a matter of semantics. Among the Pryor Mountain horses, you often see "primitive" markings—zebra stripes on the lower legs, dorsal stripes, shoulder stripes—that are highly regarded by wild-horse enthusiasts. But as Phil Sponenberg pointed out, "Primitive color doesn't mean a primitive horse. This is primitive color on a highly developed Spanish-type horse." The mustangs that multiplied across the West until they seemed almost as numerous as the buffalo were still the products of more than 5,000 years of coevolution with humans. The Spaniards who brought those horses to America were the finest horsemen—and horse breeders—of their era, and the horses they brought with them were not bred to such a high pitch of refinement by being left alone in the wilderness.

The wildness of wild horses, like the wildness of wild humans, is a metaphor. To some people it's a necessary metaphor; to others it's an encumbrance. . . .

The light had fallen, and Floyd Schwieger's band of horse watchers—the wind still in their hair and ears—had headed down the mountain the way they came, toward the lights of Lovell and the lights of the wallboard plant outside town. Four of us had picked our way along a more easterly ridge, and when the road dropped down beside a wash, we stopped. There were six young stallions in the band, six stallions traveling across the face of a shallow canyon. They crossed the wash and worked their way, one by one, up to a stud pile—a mound of droppings, a signpost, to which each of them now contributed. They were too young for the sexual contests to come, and in the growing dimness their coats—duns and roans and blacks—seemed to pick up the deepening color of the day's end. They knew where we were, and they were curious.

It was easy to cherish their freedom, hard not to love the sight of them going about their business in the elliptical way horses have—acting more like cats than like dogs. In my mind there was no question that the Pryor Mountain horses—all wild horses—deserve protection for reasons that do, finally, have as much to do with their beauty as with their genetic heritage. . . .

But seeing those stallions, watching the horses we had all seen earlier that day, riding a Spanish mustang named Montana through the mountains of California as I had done only a few weeks before, all I could feel was the fittedness of our two species and what a triumph that was, not over the wildness of horses, but over the wildness of ourselves. It was a community—the community of horses and humans—from which I did not ever want to be banished. 🙶

**N**oted for their intelligence and great stamina, wild horses have endured in spite of extremes of nature and exploitation by humans.

Following pages: **W**ild horses have acute eyesight and their hearing is sharper than that of a stabled horse.

EXCERPTED FROM *THE WOMAN AND THE HORSE* AS TOLD BY "ASSINIBOINE"

ALFRED L. KROEBER, COMPILER

# THE WOMAN WHO MARRIED THE HORSE

THE PEOPLE SENT OUT TWO young men to look for buffalo. They killed one and were butchering it. Then one of them said, "I will go to that hill and look around; do you continue to butcher." He went on the hill, and his companion went on with the butchering. The one on the hill looked about him with field glasses. At Many-Lakes he saw a large herd of wild horses. He continued to look at them. Then he saw a person among them. Then he saw something streaming behind the person. He thought it was a loose breech-cloth. He called his companion, and said to him, "Look!" Then they went nearer. They saw that it was indeed a person. They thought that it was something unnatural (*kaxtawuu*). Therefore they did not try to disturb the person, but went back. They asked the people, "Did you ever miss a person?"

An old man said, "Yes. A man once lost his wife as the camp moved. She was not found." Thereupon the young men told what they had seen. The people thought it must be this woman. The whole camp went there. All the people mounted their best horses in order to catch her. When they approached the place, they surrounded the whole country. All of them had mirrors. When they had gone all around, they turned the mirrors and reflected with them, signalling that the circle was complete. Then they drew together. The four that were mounted on the fastest horses started toward the herd. The wild horses ran, but, wherever they went, they saw people. The person in the herd was always in the lead. The people continued to close up on the horses. When they got them into a small space, they began to rope them. Six of the

*Alerted to danger, a band of mares will quickly stampede across the range.*

horses and the woman escaped. She was exceedingly swift. The people headed them off, and at last drove them into an enclosure. With much trouble they at last succeeded in fastening one rope on her leg and one on her arm. Then they picketed her at the camp like a horse. At night a young man went out. He lay down on the ground near her, looking at her. Then the woman spoke: "Listen, young man. I will tell you something. You must do what I tell you. It is the truth. Long ago the camp was moving. I was far behind. I saw a large black stallion come. He had a rope on him. I jumped off my horse and caught him, thinking he belonged to some one in camp. When I had hold of the rope, he spoke to me. He said, 'Jump on my back.' Then I climbed on him. He is the one that took me away. He is my husband. I have seven children by him, seven young horses. There is one, that gray one; there another one, that spotted one; there a black painted one; there a black one." She showed him all her children. "That is my husband," she said of a black horse that was tied near by. "I cannot go back to the tribe now. I have become a horse. Let me go. Let us all go. Tie a bell on a horse of such a color; then you will be lucky in getting horses. If you will let me loose, I will give you forty persons (you will kill forty enemies). If you do not loose me, many of the tribe will die." Then the young man went to his father and told what the woman had said. The old man went outside and cried it out to the people. Then they freed her and the horses. They ran amid flying dust, the woman far in the lead.

**A**t the time of birth, a mare is allowed to roam away from the band and seek a secluded spot to drop her foal.

*In Native American culture, the horse was the first form of property that could make a warrior rich.*

**M**ost wild horses are smaller than stable horses: wild stallions rarely exceed 1,000 pounds, and some mares weigh as little as 700 pounds.

AN ORIGINAL ESSAY BY

DAYTON O. HYDE

# THE APPY MARE

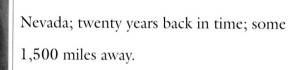

THE APPALOOSA MARE CAME crashing out of the livestock truck, pounded down the unloading chute, tried to climb the corral fence, then charged toward me, yellow teeth bared, ready to eat the world. As I scrambled over the top rail, she ripped the back pocket off my Levi's, then whirled to kick, blasting a jag of splinters out of the dry juniper logs. The old mare was shaking with stress, and so bug-eyed with rage that it would have seemed inconceivable to me that one day we would be friends.

One ear chewed off maybe by her mother in birthing, her color odd, pink warts on her nose, and an ancient bullet slash across the flat of her right hip, made me guess where I'd seen that animal before. She'd maybe come halfway across America to haunt me for something that wasn't my doing. In Northern Nevada; twenty years back in time; some 1,500 miles away.

I remember that day. I had skirted the Black Rock Desert by night, eased my horse to the sun-baked rim of Little High Rock Canyon, and sat looking down at the shine of water along the bottom, wondering if somewhere among that chaos of ancient fractured rock, there might be an animal trail leading down to the cool.

The band of wild horses came tiptoeing down off the far rimrocks, working its way silently toward water. An old black lead mare came first, stopping frequently to stare and work the canyon thermals for scent of danger. Behind her were three dry mares, equally watchful, then a mare and foal, followed by a battle-scarred blue roan stallion. The foal caught my

*Even when captured, stallions continue to defy confinement.*

eye, an Appaloosa, one ear off, rump oddly spattered with white as though a magpie had roosted there, the rest of the animal blue like sage smoke over a November campfire.

The little filly stuck to its mother's side like a bad smell, even though there was only room on the trail for one. Dislodged maybe by time, a small rock rattled and clicked down the hillside then chunked into the sun-dappled water on the canyon floor. The wild horses froze, thinking about that rock. The Appaloosa's mother restrained the foal with her nose, and, for moments, the band seemed sculpted in stone.

Suddenly, the willows along the bottom erupted in rifle fire. The stallion humped up, leaped, screamed once, and died. I shouted at the mustangs to run, but only the mare and foal made it up over the narrow trail to safety. I caught one last glimpse of the little Appaloosa as it dragged with one crippled hip after its mother, then they were lost in the sun. I roared a torrent of bad words at the horse hunters and got the hell out of there, never dreaming that I would see that filly again.

In 1988, I was buying cattle in Nevada for the family ranch in Oregon, when I passed government-sponsored feedlots near Lovelock, crowded with hundreds of captured wild horses. I had grown up riding wild horses. I had a feeling that, somehow, I was meant to help the horses escape.

I had an impulse to sneak into the feedlots in the dead of night and open all the gates, but dismissed the idea as wildly impractical. The horses had been gathered in the first place because their numbers on the range had exceeded their food supply. Releasing them wouldn't solve the problem.

Instead I headed off to find a place in the West where there was land enough and grass enough to set up a wild horse sanctuary system on private lands, so that the unadoptable wild horses languishing in feedlots could run wild and free. I had little or no money but lots of enthusiasm, and hoped that there would be some good, caring people out there who would embrace my dream and help.

I had sworn that wild horses couldn't drag me away from my beautiful ranch in Oregon, but they had. All too suddenly I left family and friends behind and set off to South Dakota to pursue my dream, to get those wild horses out of the dust, disease, and boredom of the feedlots, and let them run wild and free on better land than they had seen this century.

Tired of problems with excess wild horses, Congress embraced my plan, and soon trucks were rolling in daily bringing mustangs, most of whom had no idea of fences or that they couldn't get back to their home ranges by galloping west. It was from one of those trucks that the old Appaloosa mare bolted. The sight of her one chewed-off ear triggering my memory of the little filly I had once met so many years ago.

The BLM records on the old Appaloosa are slender indeed. "Appaloosa. Sex, Female. Captured 1987 on the Black Rock Desert in Northern Nevada. Unadoptable. Shipped by truck to the Black Hills Wild Horse Sanctuary, Hot Springs, South Dakota, from holding facilities at Bloomfield, Nebraska. Released, September 21, 1988."

I didn't see much of the old mare for a while after I opened the gate to freedom. I had three sanctuary units to manage with 1,800 wild horses, and the old App stayed up high where she could see Wyoming, as close to Nevada and her old range as she could get. She finally picked up with a Kigor mustang off the Steens Mountain range in Oregon, and I knew I had a chance to settle her down since her new friend was addicted to the grain I kept in my back of my pickup truck. Soon, the old App would follow the other mare down off the heights to fight over the pile of oats I left them as a peace offering. Once she even nickered to me but I was careful not to let her see me smile.

There is, among wild horses, an innate sense of home. Horse bands, unfortunately, tend to be too sedentary for their own good and the health of the range they occupy. When nature drys up the waterholes and scorches the grass, wild horses often fail to move on. As the land dies, the horses die with it. Years back, predators such as wolves and humans harassed the horses and drove them to new ranges, mixing up the herds so that far less inbreeding occurred.

My days on the sanctuary were soon spent playing wolf or Indian, moving the horse herds on to fresh ranges even though the horses would pace the dividing fences for days after each move, trying to return to where they had grazed before.

The mustangs had never forgotten the trauma of their capture and would get silly any time a man ahorseback or a helicopter would appear in the distance. But they would allow me to drift them afoot, or bump along behind them in my battered old pickup truck. Horses can only concentrate on one thing at a time, and I soon learned that when they were headed in the direction I wanted them to go, it was best not to distract them.

Wild horses live in a matriarchy. Each band has a lead mare who determines where to graze, when to leave for water, and how best to elude the enemy. The stallion stumbles along behind, pretending importance, mainly concerned with keeping his harem together so that no rival stallion can steal a mare. When danger threatens, the stallion trails the band, keeping between his mares and the enemy.

The groups of wild horses had been captured in Oregon, Nevada, and Wyoming, and contained a good many old mares who had once enjoyed status in their herds as lead mares. They did not give up their old habits easily.

Whenever I would attempt to drift a gathering of horses on to a different part of their range, every old lead mare would remember her past, dash through the herd in an attempt to gather a band, and lead them to safety. My herd would suddenly fragment into six different bunches, all heading at a long trot for rocky steeps where they knew I couldn't drive my pickup.

The old App, of course, was the worst. She would run through the herd with such conviction and semblance of real terror, that the others would assume that she had seen some monstrous danger, and away they would race after her, the old mare running flat out and sassy, thundering down trails only she knew about. In time they would do a big circle and end up back where we had started.

The mare and I were two generals, each with opposing battle plans. Time and again she defeated me, and left me with a day wasted, and my pickup truck severely damaged from racing forty miles an hour over a devil's garden of ancient rocks. There came a time when there was no turning her from her headlong flight. Her wispy tail would come up, her eyes would glass over just as soon as I tried to move her band, and off she would race, charging past my vehicle as though it were invisible.

It was grain that was her final undoing. Every time she sprinted off with her band, I fed the remaining horses a taste of sweet chop. It didn't take long to erode her following. The next time she went running off in pretended terror, the other mares stayed behind and soon she was the first mustang off the mountain to get to the grain.

Little by little, the wild horse herds left their fears behind and accepted my presence. Often as I wandered afoot in the darkness I could hear them near me; a flinty hoof striking rock perhaps, sounding a blunt bell. Often, far down a ridge, a lonely mare nickered for a friend separated, somehow, by the night's grass-to-grass wanderings, and maybe a black shape nearest me would answer back.

In any dawn, the moment comes suddenly when the white horses in the herd take first shape, like scattered blobs of remnant moonlight. Palominos and light buckskins, sorrels and roans, then bays and blacks. The herds themselves take form in the pinkish dawn. I can almost read horse thoughts as grazing buddies come together at the edge of the herd and drift away together like human couples leaving a bar at midnight hoping others won't notice and follow.

The old App rises from where she has been lying down, stretches the stiffness from ancient limbs, and picks her way down through the rocks where I have put out grain. In a horse herd there is no respect for age. Younger horses have followed my every movement and dash in to fight each other. The old mare goes back to her ridge unfed.

But the old lady figures it out. The next morning and the next she anticipates my route and meets me in a valley screened from the others where she can have her own ration of grain and dine in peace.

There is not much fun and games in old mustang mares. During the summer they have given all their extra energy to provide milk to demanding foals who have clung to their sides like shadows on a sunny day. In vain the foals have tried to tease the mares into playing games. Now the youngsters begin to socialize. They race each other across the prairie, the rocky, arid ground beating hardness into tiny hooves, leaping gullys, prancing, dancing, pawing over backs, acting silly, tails high, fair to bursting with energy.

Playing hard, they chew on each others' manes, rising together in a juvenile waltz, cavorting like quarreling stallions, backing into each other to drum a tattoo of hoofbeats on the other's ribs.

In November, shortly after midnight, a group of wild horses comes down from the rimrock, slipping in so silently I do not hear them come. I look out my window to see the old App, ghoulish in the moonlight, standing watch as the others move through piney moonshadows to drink.

Gone from their coats is the sleekness of summer. Already these lovers of the storm are jacketed for zero. The first snows will pile on them unmelting until blacks, bays, paints, roans, grullas, and sorrels will vanish white on white. There is so much shelter here of pine and rock, but give the mustangs a good blizzard and they seek out the highest hills, standing just below the crest, turning tail to the buffeting winds, each taking its turn at the windy edge of the herd.

There are no flies in winter to plague the mustangs and each horse's tail hangs like a plumb bob, at rest until spring, except to register, perhaps, a swish of anger when another animal ventures too close.

I take the old App a big round bale of hay and place it for her where the others cannot see. For a time, she watches from a distant hillside, then curiosity brings her close. Lured by a tantalizing odor of summer, she bites at the bale and jerks out a long beard of grass. In her lifetime grass has never behaved thus and she whirls in terror. Unable to open her mouth and release the grass, she thunders away, bucking and striking, until at last the beard falls to the ground. She stops at a distance, and gradually works her way back to the fallen clump, sniffing it carefully. Now it is in a more familiar form and she finishes every last wisp.

Soon she is back at the bale, willing to try again. Another wisp of hay and she whirls off, but the distance is shorter now. Some thirty feet out, she drops the hay, then eats it on the ground. Later that afternoon I pass that way again and she is still there, head buried in the bale as though she had been raised on such easy fare. Winters are long and hard. The old App saves her energy and makes no motions not necessary to her survival.

Spring peers around the corner, smiles, then retreats. Like domestic horses, the mustangs are quick to sense meaning-ful change in the weather, galloping wild and free down mountainsides, across gullys, splashing noisily through meltwater rivers, hooves making the first thunder of the season across the hollow drum of the plains.

A bunch of wild horses traveling generates its own music. There is not only the drumming of hooves, but whinnying—of foals for their mothers, mothers for foals, and one friend for another, the challenge of one distant stallion to a fancied rival. There are softer sounds, too, the cough from a dusty lung or the contented snuffling horses make when life goes well.

This spring, the pasque flowers turn the rocky hillsides along the Cheyenne River to purple. Most of the wild horses move high to sandy ridges where the blackroot grows. Ancient Indians led their winter-weak horses to these same ridges, and, in three weeks, they were ready for the warpath.

The old App stays behind. Once or twice she ventures to the edge of the spring-swollen river and looks across with longing as though to follow the others to the high places she has loved ever since she came here. She waits for me every morning, listening for the rattle and squeak of my truck as I head off through the pines to give her grain. Her nostrils flare as she approaches, and she snorts like the blast of an old musket, unwilling to dispense her friendship lightly. I would feel better if her acceptance of me were not bought with grain. She tiptoes forward, then whirls and trots down the hillside. It is an act she must put on every morning out of pride.

Her tail is a disgrace. Never long and full, it is wispy like her mane but nevertheless clogged with burs from wild licorice

and burdock. Flies cluster on her back, just out of reach of her club. She is so close now I can see every nose wart, every blemish on her hide. The ancient bullet crease across the top of her hip has formed a ridge of hard horn as though some excess hoof material has oozed up like lava through a fissure in her body.

There is meaning in her aloneness. I can read the signs. The old mare hardly touches her grain and she stands listless, eyes sunken. She won't be here tomorrow. She has already picked her spot to die, beneath a gnarled old juniper overlooking the range she came to love. She will spend her last hours there standing alone. At best, my ministrations of grain have brought her a couple of extra years of the good life.

High on the ridges above Cheyenne, I see wild horses running in pure joy. I think of that old Appy mare, and I smile. 〞

**T**he wild Appaloosa of the High Plateau benefited from good feed and a mild climate, resulting in a taller stature—some were fifteen hands tall.

**O**nly a few hundred pure-blooded descendants of the sixteenth-century Spanish stock survive today, salvaged from the wild. They are in captivity in special registries in North and South America. The blood of these rare horses still flows in the veins of scattered wild-horse bands throughout the West.

**A**ll determination and fighting muscle, the wild horse is a worthy opponent of any cowboy.

EXCERPTED FROM *A THOUSAND MILES OF MUSTANGIN'* BY

BEN K. GREEN

# MUSTANGIN'

I HAD BEEN OBSERVANT ALL day as to my direction and location of the sun and when the shadows were pretty long and I had begun to wonder if I might spend the night away from camp because I was too dumb to find it, I saw a band of nice, fat, solid colored, good kind of horses in a little grassy spot at the bottom of a canyon. They were too far for me to get to them and get back that day but I sure was glad to know there was at least one band of wild horses in those mountains.

I turned Beauty in what I believed to be the right general direction, and as I had done many times before to give her a complete signal of what we were up against, I reached up and pulled her bridle off and tied it to the saddle horn. She knew when I did that that I was lost. She let her head down and ate a few bites of tall gamma grass and then raised her head and looked around and made about a half turn back to the right, the direction I had just come from and in a good straight steady walk without any looking back or looking around or showing any signs of human mix-up, climbed up over a point in the mountains and dropped back to the left about 200 yards and I could see the spring in my camp four or five miles on the other side of the slope in front of us. I never apologized or pushed her or said a word and hoped she wouldn't tell anybody else when I was unsaddling her next to the spring.

I spent the next two or three days getting closer to this band of wild horses and began to see enough

*Wild-horse herds that stampeded ranchers' cattle and stole remuda horses held little romance for the hardworking cowpuncher.*

of them to know that they weren't branded and to know that they were sure enough mustangs. They were a little bigger and a little better quality in their feet and legs due to their mountain home than the ones I had caught in the Big Bend. It was about the third day that I waited by a place where they were watering on the creek with the wind blowing against me so that they wouldn't smell me until they came in to water. I was a little over anxious and as they began to turn back from drinking, I made a wild run into them and caught a nice fat mare that proved to have a little age on her and was sure mean to fight.

I had a four-strand silk manila lariat rope on her that she couldn't break, but she would run at my horse with her mouth open and we would have to dodge her and get her tangled up in the rope or she would turn back real quick again. I managed to get her wrapped around a tree and me to have the longest end of the rope and I got down and started to her head to put a hackamore on her. She was choking pretty bad and had rolled her eyes around and was watching me real close. In the split half second that it takes to slip the nosepiece over a horse's head is when she snapped my right hand. I pulled as quick as I could and she tore the skin about two and a half or three inches on the bottom and not quite that much with her top teeth, but I was jerking enough that she didn't bite a whole plug out of the back of my hand.

I decided there wasn't much point in worrying about whether she choked or not and I got on my horse. I was riding the big stout young bay horse that was green-broke when I left home and didn't mind putting some abuse on him, and me and him managed to wrap her some around that tree. I maneuvered my horse around and pitched the rope over her rump a time or two as I unwrapped her from that tree without giving her any slack. The choking for air had helped her disposition a little and she didn't make another run at us. All the other horses were clear out of sight and I drove, rather than dragged, this mare as much as I could and she was smart. She caught on pretty fast that dragging is when she choked and drive is when she could get her breath.

I got her to camp a little before dark and wrapped her around another tree and left the bay horse holding her. Then I saddled Beauty and roped and jerked her hind feet out from under which layed her on the ground straightened out. She already had me on notice that she was bad so I let them stretch and choke her while I put a hackamore on her and tied it to the tree. I slipped the lariat rope off of her head and got back away from her. Then I spoke to Beauty to step up and when she struggle to get up off the ground, she naturally kicked her back feet from the loop on that rope.

I had a fair smear of blood all over me and my clothes from this bite she had put on me and unsaddled both horses and went down to the spring and began to try to wash up. I didn't have anything much to doctor my hand with and I started to put a little bit of iodine on it. I realized there is no such thing as a little bit of iodine and knew it would burn those open gashes pretty bad so I washed it off good and greased it with a salty meat rind which has always been a good cowboy remedy. I thought to myself that in the clean high dry mountain air that it would probably get well without much doctoring. This was my roping hand and next morning it was so swelled and stiff that I couldn't rope with it. I messed around camp and played with what gentle horses I had and walked by occasionally and kicked a little dirt at that old bay bitin' mare and didn't really care too much if she had broke her neck, but her kind don't have much bad happen to them.

About the third day my fist was about the size of a Texas grapefruit and I could barely stand to get my sleeve over it. The oldest of the whiteheaded Yaqui Indians came to camp that day, and I made a few signs and showed him my hand. He drew me a map on the ground with a small limb and marked a house and made enough signs and talked enough to make me understand that there was a doctor there. At least that's what I thought he said. I got on a horse and found the place in about three hours ride and rode up to the yard gate of a little 'dobe hut and hollered hello.

There was a real old dried up Mexican woman, maybe part Indian, came to the door. She didn't speak but walked out to the crude rock fence that separated the yard from the rest of the world. I thought I would show her my hand and she would tell me where the doctor was. She looked at my hand and showed no sign of sympathy or asked how it happened or anything of the sort. She finally asked me if I had any white flour. I told her I did back in camp. Then she asked about some yeast, or at least I thought she meant yeast. I didn't have any yeast but I had some sourdough that worked all the time in a jar that I carried with me to make sourdough biscuits. She told me to get the flour and the yeast.

I rode pretty straight and made good time because my hand had begun to hurt bad and red streaks were running up my arm from it. When I got back to her house, it was nearly dark and I though she was going to do something right away to help my hand. She took the flour and the sourdough yeast and made sort of a wet paste out of it, not near as thick as dough. She poured this out on a flat rock and turned an old glass goblet with the stem broken off, making sure that this watery paste sealed around the glass. Then she told me three days from now that the medicine would be strong.

I wondered whether I would have a hand left in another three days but I laid around camp and bathed my hand in the spring and held it up to where it wouldn't throb quite so bad. The third morning I was at her 'dobe house by daylight. She waited until the sun came up and went out to the flat rock in her yard, and the goblet turned bottom side up had grown full of mold from the dough. She lifted the goblet and took her finger and wiped about a third of the dough and mold out from the glass and smeared it over the two raw reddish blue places on my hand. She made enough signs to make me understand that I would have to wait until nearly sundown and put it on again. I layed around under a big shade in her yard and she brought me some pretty hard kind of grub at noon and my arm began to get easy. My hand may not have been going down but it had quit swelling. She cleaned the place off good and doctored it again and wiped the rest of this mess up and wrapped it in a green dagger cactus leaf and said that would keep it moist. She told me to use it tomorrow and she would make some more medicine.

In about three days and the second goblet full of this treatment, my hand had gone down and there were protective scabs forming over the open places and I was able to go back to using my arm to handle and rope and work horses. Here was the making of penicillin in its first and crudest form and I was too dumb, as I guess thousands of other people had been, to recognize what the old medicine women knew would cure infection.

I offered to pay the old medicine woman, but she didn't want any money and said she could sure use some flour. I knew that these people lived on cornmeal because most of them raised their corn and they could rarely afford to buy white flour. I had bought some small sacks of flour at the commissary because I could pack them better than one big sack so the next day I took her a ten-pound sack of flour. She was sure happy to get the flour and made motions and signs and told me she would eat a little bit of it and keep the rest for medicine.

I managed to ride enough during the time that my hand was bad to keep my horses pretty well on a little range bordering up and down the stream and around the mountain that I was camped on. Next day I pushed them all in close to the camp and left them still loose and free to graze and started back to the canyon where I caught that last old bitin' mare. This band of horses weren't too badly scared from me catchin' that one mare and hadn't moved range.

As best I could tell there were about thirty head of mares and most of them had colts that had been born that spring. The stud was a seal-brown horse with a small star in its face and no white markings on his feet and a little bit larger than mustangs usually are. He didn't seem to have a whole lot of fear of one rider and he would put his mares in a protective spot but he had no fear of coming out and meeting me which made me think he might be kin to that old mare I caught. There's no horse or nobody horseback anxious to have a fight with a range stud and this was making it pretty hard to figure out a way to get close enough to his mares to catch any of them.

I rode for several days moving these horses around but they always stayed in the foothills and never did get themselves in a bad spot where I'd have a chance to trap or rope one of them. I guess I had spent about a week at this kind of foolishness when one morning about daylight the old Yaqui Indian and two more about his age showed up at my camp before breakfast. I fixed them a big pot of coffee and fried them some flour tortillas and fed them on salt pork bacon and refried beans. When I about had breakfast ready, I thought I would make a hit with these old boys. I still had a few cans of cream corn that I had brought from the commissary so I poured it in on top of the beans while they were fryin' and stirred it all together. We had a few words along while I was fixin' breakfast and they sat by the fire and drank coffee.

That bunch of old chiefs sure did give that cream corn and fried beans a fit and bragged on the coffee but they weren't too fond of that old salty fat sowbelly, but they didn't have anything on me—I wasn't too fond of it either. They sat and smoked their pipes a little while, and I sat and watched them knowing if they had a proposition they would bring it up and it wouldn't do any good if I propositioned them anyway. After a while one of them spoke up and said, "One mare make you cripple. How you think you catch whole band?"

I thought that was funny and laughed and looked at my sore hand and said, "I'm willing to learn from the Yaqui. Is there a better way to catch these horses?" 🦶🦶

**A** *stallion will communicate his displeasure with threatening behavior: grotesque elongations of his neck and rhythmic weaving back and forth of his head which is generally held low, almost to the ground.*

**C***owboys, on more than one occasion, have been severely bitten and savagely kicked by wild mustangs when attempting to capture them.*

AN ORIGINAL ESSAY BY

LAURA BELL

# FERAL HEART

MORNING SPILLS ACROSS THE ridges like paint tipped over, its fingers of pale light reaching through the sage to flush from the leaves the cries of small birds. From a ragged spine of rock, my knot of a thousand sheep begins to loosen as, one by one, the ewes and lambs trickle off the edges in search of fresh feed. The air is awake, alive with movement. It is May, spring in northern Wyoming, and I am camped on the high benches of the McCullough Peaks.

At the edge of camp, my dogs sit on their haunches and lean out into the morning with a working dog's earnest air of responsibility. Lady is red heeler, slight and speckled. A veteran queen of sheepcamp. Louise is blue merle Aussie shepherd, younger, and owner of one blue eye that speaks of righteousness. Today, it says, sheep are leaving the bedground and your horse isn't saddled. We're ready. Send us. Their faces turn in quick attention from sheep to Willy eating his morning grain to me, coffee still in hand.

Picketed in a small clearing off from camp, Willy stands with his nose shoved deeply into his bucket of oats. I gather my saddle up from underneath the sheepwagon and pack it to him, heaving it to his back with a grunt. "Next life I'll be a tall woman," I say and pull the cinch up loose under his belly. Abruptly, his head swings up through the air, startled at some intrusion into the landscape. He stands frozen, watching so intently that for a moment he forgets to chew.

It's the horses that he sees, slipping down along the rim of the narrow canyon that falls from the peaks, widening and softening to spill into green feed below

*The ultimate growth of individual horses in the wild herds corresponds to the food available on the open range.*

our camp. It's the bay stallion's band, one of three feral bands that range in the McCullough Peaks and whose paths we cross from time to time, sharing, as we do, the neighborhood.

They step lightly down the rim, coming closer to our camp and the sheep now streaming off the hill. There are seven mares, mostly bays and sorrels, two spring colts, and the stallion, moving off to the side of the group and slightly in its lead. Among them, there is no one animal that I would call beautiful. They are small and dense and rough, the shape of their bones buried under coats ragged still with winter. Like the gnarled firs that lean from the winds at timberline, these horses are carved by the elements in which they live, not by any breeder's idea of beauty.

Still, you should see them move. All grace and ease they make their way with full attention, their noses weaving through the air to catch our scent. Coming closer, they move like dancers seasoned side by side, their tough bodies one single expression of elegance, their effort one single chord of survival.

I have watched them bear a storm. With butts turned windward and heads hung low, they shift their warm weight into each other and stand through whatever the skies pour out to them. From the comfort of my sheepwagon stove, I have watched them bear a storm and found my pity grown to envy. Of their loyalty. Of their dependence on each other. Of the sureness it allows them in a landscape that does so little to shelter.

This morning they stop just above camp, not fifty yards from us, at the edge of the hungry wave of bleating sheep. The stallion stands with head high, watching Willy who watches him. About the mares, there is an air both wary and curious. Almost playful. One colt minces forward to sniff a woolly fleece, then leaps back from the surprise of it, stirring the mares into a ripple of snorts and skittering bucks. The stallion ducks his head, too, and shakes it in our direction like a dare. Unbearably tempted, Willy charges the end of his picket chain with a squeal.

A year ago they took him, called him away with whatever power their freedom holds. It had been a wilder, Marchy, morning with winds gusting against the flimsy tin of my sheepwagon roof. I woke to Willy, white-eyed and snorting, strained against his picket line that was snaked in a tangle through the brush. Following his eyes to the low hills above camp, I saw his torment in the three wild bands that had gathered in the coming storm to show out for each other, to strut in the electrical currents of air sweeping in from the northern skies. The hills were charged with their movement, the stallions circling and swinging, heads and tails high in the wind, around the edges of their mares. Willy was changed by his awareness of them, no longer the familiar member of my family, and I knew he would be gone if not for the chain that held him in camp.

So, I was careful as I saddled him. I led him away from camp to get on, but he reared and ducked his head, and because I was too stubborn to follow, the bridle slid from his head to the ground. For a moment, he stood between the two worlds, his eyes to the hills, one ear twitching slightly to the rattle of the oat bucket and the grain sifting through my fingers. With the stiff-legged staccato movements of exhilaration, he was gone, stirrups flapping like wings, into the hills. With his approach, the horses stirred into a rumble of confusion and disappeared, finally, over the ridge with Willy among them.

I remember standing for a long time watching the empty

hills, awed that my life could change so in a moment. No phone to call with, no neighbor to flag down. Only a spidery track of dusty road whose miles would soon be impassable with the storm. I remember looking at my dogs and wondering if it were possible for them, too, to be drawn away from me by some experience more primally "dog." I thought not, and wondered at the difference in Willy that took him away.

I celebrated my twenty-fifth birthday on foot in the rain the next day, tearing a soggy tuna fish sandwich in pieces for Lady and Louise. For six days it rained, and on the seventh, my camp-tender chugged into camp at dawn chained up on all fours to get through the mud, worried about what he might find when he got there. Willy had been found out by the highway, lonesome and cut up and looking for oats. As a gelding, he'd had no place with the wild horses and had been fought out of the bands by the stallions. Through the back-range grapevine, John had gotten the news and showed up at first light with a spare horse loaded in the stockrack and an aging birthday cake on the front seat beside him.

That was a year ago. If Willy has memories of the beating he suffered, they are paled by the sparks and snorts flying across the distance this morning. Heads are up, and eyes are bright. In an air charged with invitation, I hang my weight into his head to draw him down, my own memories all too vivid. I turn to the horses up the hill, their spirits like bright lights beckoning, and realize that I, too, want to be gone away. More than anything else. More than the caution of my isolation. More than the wisdom of my losses. I want to shake my head back at them. I want to dare.

I fasten the bridle over his head and pull the cinch tight around his belly. Cheeking his head around to me, I dance his dance, pulling myself, finally, up into the saddle. Do we dare? In a sideways prance, we step gingerly into the sage, and the horses' heads fly high, their ragged manes catching the wind.

Can we dare not on a morning in spring run with our hearts stretched wide? And so I lean only slightly, shifting my weight to give him his head, and we are gone, hard and fast and wild through the sage toward the horses, already bolted and bucking up the hill. One hand a clutch of mane and reins, the other anchored to the horn, I pledge myself on for the ride, dogs yipping madly through the brush behind us. Below us the ground falls away unevenly and leaves us stumbling through the air over sage and rock and the holes of prairie dogs. I lose my sight to wind and tears and close my body around the center of what there is to trust and trust it.

For long moments, we ride their wake of dust and drumming hooves, suspended in the balance of fear and grace as hooves meet ground and the ground holds us up. As though there is no choice, we follow until our lungs and hearts can stand no more. Glittering and heaving, we pull up to watch them take the ridge. They snort and jump and stamp their feet at us, disappearing over the top with necks snaking and heads shaking in triumph.

Turning back, the morning is spread before us, raw and brilliant, tumbling for miles down to the desert basin below. The sheep are fanned in a great pale arc through the sage, and the birds cry out their morning songs. With corks popped off our sedated hearts, we fall from the slope, changed, and pick our trail back to camp and the rituals of our day.

An Original Essay by

Lynne Bama

# ROUNDUP!

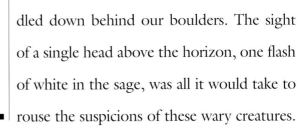

WE CROUCHED BEHIND ROCKS on the spine of the hill, looking out at the buttes and benches, tilting mesas, and far-off mountain ranges of northwestern Wyoming. The highest peaks were dusted with the first snowfall of September.

The only signs of human presence here were two lines of jute fencing that converged into a break in the ridge to our left. Hidden in the draw behind us was a metal corral with a loading chute at one end. Two stock trucks were parked nearby, and I could hear a U.S. Bureau of Land Management official talking to a helicopter pilot on his two-way radio.

Soon the faint throb of the distant aircraft came in on a whiff of breeze that sighed through the cured grasses of the outcrop. It faded, then returned, louder and closer. We could hear it swinging back and forth behind its prey. As it surged above the horizon we hud-dled down behind our boulders. The sight of a single head above the horizon, one flash of white in the sage, was all it would take to rouse the suspicions of these wary creatures.

With a sudden pounding of hooves, the three cowboys who had been waiting near the trap hurtled into view, yelling. And then twenty-two wild horses flew past us on the dead run, bunched tightly, their long, shaggy manes and tails flying. Although their untrimmed fetlocks made them seem heavy-footed, they hurtled down the steep pitch that led to the trap with grace and power.

We were getting up from our hiding places when there were warning shouts. The helicopter was still out there, pushing. Finally a last small colt staggered into view, exhausted. One of the wranglers wheeled back out and led it down the hill.

**A** *stallion will put himself in front of danger to give his mares lead time in which to escape.*

But as we spectators straggled down the slope to the trap, we could see that something was wrong. At first I didn't notice the black horse lying at the head of the corral, just in front of the chute. Even after I saw it, I didn't immediately realize that it was dead. But there was an unmistakable silence around it. The other horses in the corral stood as far away from the body as they could. The people huddled in little groups, not talking much. Some of them looked angry.

"What happened?" I asked the nearest official. He told me that a stallion, running at the head of the bunch, had entered the trap full speed, slammed into the gate, and broken its neck.

The general feeling among the people there—both spectators and officials—was that the horse had done it on purpose. He was far out in front of the others, and could easily have stopped. But it's a stallion's style to bully his way through obstacles. Did he realize that failure would mean death? I wondered. Was this a kind of suicide? Nobody seemed willing to exclude that possibility.

As I looked at the inert black form behind the fence, I had the uneasy feeling that something dimly remembered was struggling to emerge. The stallion was like an artifact from a lost civilization, or a hieroglyph in a forgotten language. I no longer understood what it meant, but I knew it came from long ago. As a preadolescent girl, I had been horse crazy. When I doodled around the edges of my school notebooks, the pictures were always of stallions with arched necks and wind-tossed manes. I read every horse book I could lay my hands on, collected horse figurines, and badgered my parents into letting me take riding lessons. I never became much of a rider, though. Sitting on a horse was not what really interested me: in my deepest soul, I wanted to *be* a horse.

It was obvious to my ten-year-old self that horses were not only stronger and faster and more beautiful than people; their relationship to the earth was also cleaner and more direct. They did not kill other animals for food or clutter up the landscape with subdivisions. All they needed was grass and water and open space.

The life of a wild horse seemed like an ideal existence. And if I could have chosen a horse to be, it would not have been one of the tame creatures I climbed onto each week at the riding academy, but Walter Farley's black stallion.

By the time I was thirteen or fourteen, I had resigned myself to going through life in the lesser form I had been born in, and the whole fantasy evaporated. Or so I had thought. But now, forty years and several thousand miles away from that childhood, as the wild horses had shot past me into the trap, I was startled to realize that I was crying.

It was plain, however, that whatever was stirring back to life in my mind was only going to cause trouble here. This roundup had already been delayed once by appeals from animal rights groups, which is probably why the BLM had allowed spectators. But it was subtly apparent that the cowboys, whose eyes never quite met ours, did not like having an audience. Capturing wild horses is a tricky job at best, and with all these people watching they couldn't even curse.

I wondered if they thought we were bad luck. On an earlier run, a stallion had broken out through the jute fencing and escaped, possibly because someone hadn't hidden well enough. And now an unusual fatal accident had chagrined this team that had worked together on roundups all over the West.

There was a long delay. I didn't find out until later that when the stallion hit the fence, a mare that was already loaded on the waiting truck had reared, struck her head, and fallen. Until she got up again, the wranglers were afraid they had a second casualty as well. Finally one of the cowboys backed a vehicle up to the corral, hooked a chain around a hind leg of the dead stud, and dragged it away in a cloud of dust so the other horses could be loaded. After they were all on the trucks, I drove out to the highway between two loads of them. Where the pavement began, and we went our separate ways, I caught one last glimpse of bright eyes and pricked ears through the slats, and wondered what their fates would be.

Four years later, I still don't know how I feel about what I saw that day, so difficult is it to come to terms with the fantasy horses that continue their subterranean existence in my mind. The intellect that has grown over and obliterated them is a cool, dispassionate entity. It has all the facts about these animals. It knows that they evolved in North America, only to vanish from it around 8,000 years ago, perhaps because they were too-easy prey for human hunters. It realizes that this semiarid Wyoming landscape is no longer adapted to their solid hooves and close-cropping teeth, and accepts the inarguable logic that because there is a watershed to think of, and other wildlife, their numbers must occasionally be thinned. But I realize now that, like a foundation stone buried at the roots of my character, the horse is still there. Occasionally it will put in an appearance in a dream. Sometimes these midnight animals take on sumptuous curves and luscious colors. They rear and gambol, and there is lightning in their manes. Or I ride the black stallion at a headlong gallop through the moonlit woods. When my sister was dying of cancer, I saw a horse lying among the stones of a riverbed, one foreleg twitching slightly.

I suspect I'm not the only one who carries this substratum. What I remember most about the roundup was a pervasive sense of unease—the careful, conciliatory manner of the officials, the sullen reserve of the cowboys, the silence of the spectators. The atmosphere would not have been the same if the animals involved had been antelope or elk.

Not long ago I drove past the scene of the roundup. It was early morning, and a wintry fog had just burned off, leaving the barbed wire fences furred with ice crystals, the occasional cottonwood tree an impossible explosion of white. Some miles to the east, in a flat expanse near a great butte, the darker bodies of a band of wild horses were clearly visible against the frost-rimmed landscape. About twenty-five of them—blacks, bays, pintos, and paints, a few palominos—were drifting slowly eastward, grazing as they went, turned broadside against the warming rays of the sun.

Watching them, I remembered something the BLM official who was in charge of the roundup told me afterward. He said that on the very first day they had caught a young paint stallion, who came in with his mane and tail flying, shining in the sun. The animal was so beautiful, he said, that he had turned him loose again. Maybe, I thought, he was among the band I was watching now. At least, one part of me wanted to think so.

No matter what the logical mind says, I am comforted to see that the roots of my psyche are not just abstractions, but are still out there on the solid ground, eating its grass, rolling in its dust, sleeping stretched out on it under the sky. ,,

*Gentling some wild horses often proves unsuccessful.*

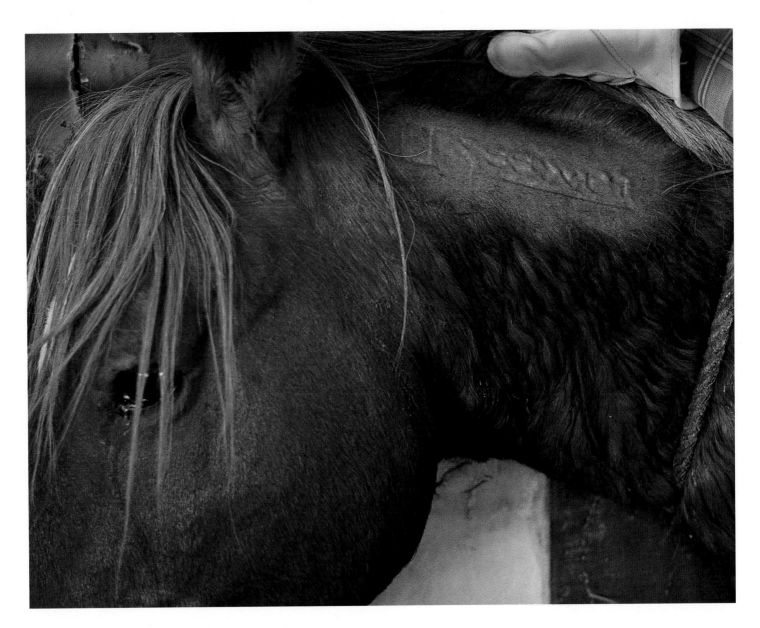

*Once tattooed with an identification number, some wild horses are then released into sanctuaries where they live out their lives.*

**F**ighting can result in bites and crushed ribs to bystanding mares  when stomping and kicking stallions lunge at each other.

# CONTRIBUTORS

**Mark Spragg** is a screenwriter, essayist, and short story writer. Recipient of the Wyoming Arts Fellowship, his stories have appeared in *Quest*, *Gray's Sporting Journal*, and *Northern Lights*. Spragg was raised in Wyoming and grew up with horses, working with his father as a guide and outfitter. He has worked as a screenwriter for Warner Brothers, Disney, TriStar, and Carolco and has just completed his first novel and a collection of essays and short stories.

**Charles M. Russell** was a brilliant illustrator, painter, and sculptor. His forty years in the West were spent as cowboy and itinerant artist. His art depicts most aspects of range and Indian life and his published writings, often illustrated with his own artwork, include informal letters and humorous anecdotes, informative essays, and Indian tales.

**Lynne Bama** has lived in northwestern Wyoming since 1968. Her writing has appeared in numerous publications, including *Sierra*, *Orion*, and *High Country News*. She is currently working on a novel.

**J. Frank Dobie** gained his literary reputation as a skilled folklorist and western nature writer. The author of numerous books, Dobie was a natural historian and an astute observer of animal life, human and otherwise. He is credited, during his tenure as university professor, with legitimizing the study of western regional literature.

**Dayton O. Hyde** is the author of eleven books and the recipient of numerous environmental awards. He is the founder and manager of the Black Hills Wild Horse Sanctuary in the Black Hills of South Dakota.

**Ben K. Green** had a lifelong career with horses and horsemen beginning with his first horse trade in the third grade. His numerous books were spellbinding yarns, drawn from the wealth of his experiences and his years as a veterinarian in southwest Texas. Green was recognized as one of the world's greatest horse experts. He raised horses and wrote on his ranch in Cumby, Texas.

**Laura Bell** has worked on sheep and cattle ranches and been a range conservator for the Forest Service. She recently was awarded a literary fellowship from the state of Wyoming and is currently working on a collection of stories. She lives and works near Salt Lake City, Utah.

**Verlyn Klinkenborg** is the author of several books including *The Last Fine Time* and *Making Hay*. He is a teacher of creative writing and is a frequent contributor and an editor for *Audubon*.

# PHOTOGRAPHERS

**Michael H. Francis**, Billings, Montana: pp. 9, 21, 25, 27, 30-31, 36, 42-43, 54-55, 81, 84-85, 71, 90, 91, 94, 96-97, 87, 82, 70, 50, 75, 78-79, 67, 106-107.

**Tom & Pat Leeson**, Vancouver, Washington: pp. 22, 88-89.

**Gary Leppart**, Billings, Montana: pp. 4-5, 12, 20, 26, 28, 29, 32, 37, 41, 44-45, 58-59, 61, 81, 100-101, 109.

**Londie G. Padelsky**, Mammoth Lakes, California: pp. 8, 40, 76-77, 68-69, 98.

**John Running**, Flagstaff, Arizona: pp. 14-15, 47, 48-49, 86, 92-93, 95.

**Phil Schofield**, Bellingham, Washington: pp. 1, 18-19, 34-35, 65, 112, 113, 116-117.

**David Stoecklein**, Ketchum, Idaho: pp. Cover, 6-7, 17, 38-39, 72-73, 80, 102-103, 105.

**Rita and Charles Summers**, Aurora, Colorado: pp. 2-3, 13, 16, 46, 52, 53, 56, 57, 60, 62-63, 74, 199, 104, 108, 110-111, 114, 115.

**Dewey Vanderhoff**, Cody, Wyoming: pp. 118, 119.

**Keith Walklet**, Yosemite, California: pp. 24.

**Michael Wicks**, Hailey, Idaho: pp. 33, 64, 66, 83.

GAYLORD R